BACKYARD BIRDS

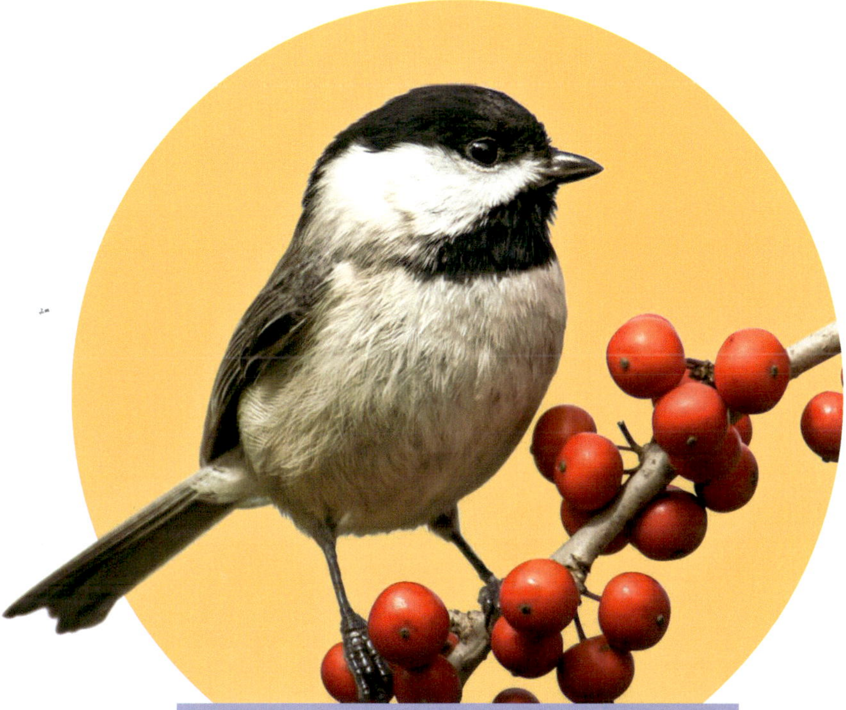

CHICKADEES

by Anastasia Suen

bib

beak

Look for these words and pictures as you read.

chicks

feeder

Have you seen this bird?
It is a chickadee.
This bird says its name.

bib

These birds are gray and white.
They have a black head.
They also have a black bib.

beak

A sharp beak cuts a tree.
It makes a hole for a nest.

Some birds use a nest box.
They lay eggs inside.
The eggs have brown spots.

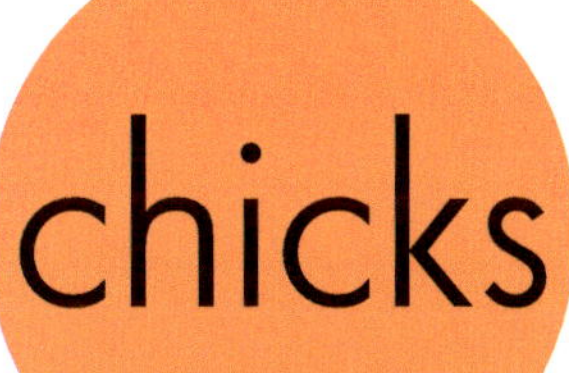

Chicks can eat bugs.
Soon they will eat berries.
They will eat seeds.

feeder

It is hard to find
food in the winter.
Birds go to a feeder.
They eat seeds.

A chickadee is a backyard bird.
Have you seen it?

bib
These birds are gray and white.
They have a black head.
They also have a black bib.
beak
A sharp beak cuts a tree.
It makes a hole for a nest.
bib
beak
Did you find?
chicks
feeder
chicks
Chicks can eat bugs.
Soon they will eat berries.
They will eat seeds.
feeder
It is hard to find
food in the winter.
Birds go to a feeder.
They eat seeds.

Spot is published by Amicus Learning, an imprint of Amicus
P.O. Box 227, Mankato, MN 56002
www.amicuspublishing.us

Library of Congress Cataloging-in-Publication Data
Names: Suen, Anastasia author
Title: Chickadees / by Anastasia Suen.
Description: Mankato, MN : Amicus Learning, an imprint of Amicus, [2026] | Series: Spot backyard birds | Audience: Ages 4-7 | Audience: Grades K-1 | Summary: "Chickadees are small black and white birds found across North America. This search-and-find book reinforces new vocabulary words with simple facts and compelling photographs to teach kindergarten and first grade readers about backyard birds"— Provided by publisher.
Identifiers: LCCN 2025010584 (print) | LCCN 2025010585 (ebook) | ISBN 9798892008310 library binding | ISBN 9798892008976 paperback | ISBN 9798892009638 ebook
Subjects: LCSH: Chickadees—Juvenile literature
Classification: LCC QL696.P2615 S84 2026 (print) | LCC QL696.P2615 (ebook) | DDC 598.8/24—dc23/eng/20250722
LC record available at https://lccn.loc.gov/2025010584
LC ebook record available at https://lccn.loc.gov/2025010585

Printed in United States of America

Ana Brauer, editor
Deb Miner, series designer
Sara Hood, book designer and photo researcher

Photos by Alamy Stock Photo/Gary Luhm / DanitaDelimont, 2, 7, 15, Ross Knowlton Nature Photography, 2, 10-11, 15; Getty Images/Schon, 6, 15, Teresa Kopec, 14, yckim98 / Imazins, 3; Shutterstock/Connie Barr, 1, Mircea Costina, 2, 12-13, 15, Oleg Mayorov, 8-9, Saeedatun, cover, 16, Wirestock Creators, 2, 4-5, 15